Excellent Exposure Photography: Start Exposure Photography Today, Even If You've Never Tried Before (A Beginner's Guide)

Table of Contents

Introduction 5

Tools of the Trade...8

Film Photography 13

Black and White Photography Versus Color....................................15

Parts of a Camera...18

Techniques..26

Full Spectrum, Light Field Photography, and More...........................28

Science and the Camera..33

Exposure Photography..36

Introduction

As children, we often recall sitting at our grandparent's homes looking at photographs of our parents taken during their childhood. If we were lucky, we may have the privilege of seeing our grandparent's parent's images captured on film, though those photographs may be in black and white. Inside these photo albums exists an intricate story of one's heritage. Those who enjoy tracing his or her ancestry could easily flip through the pages and discover the story of his or her origins. Yet, as society developed and progressed, we as individuals sought out less and less information on our pasts and looked strictly at the future. We began taking photos for the purpose of telling our story—not for posterity, but for pure intrinsic gain. This led to near catastrophic societal events.

Vanity. It is one of human nature's most prevalent sins. Vanity is a sin according to the Torah, the Qu'ran, the Bible, and other religious works. Vanity is said to have led to the fall of Satan or the devil as he viewed himself with the same superiority of God. Having a superiority complex, which is nothing more than a scientific sounding name that psychologists have given the word *vanity*, is seen as a defense mechanism. It is meant to conceal feelings of inadequacy and inferiority. Alfred Adler, who was the one who came up with the term, has had to defend his theory. Many argued that a person could not have a superiority complex *and* an inferiority complex at the same time. The argument was that a person with a true superiority complex was egotistical and believed that he or she was truly superior to others, but Adler argued that those beliefs came from a deep seated feeling of inadequacy and inferiority. Those who suffered from clinical vanity, as it were, often purchased expensive items and other possessions to maintain the appearance of being elite. Often, these people seek out those with less means for the sole purpose of extorting their meagerness and capitalizing on their adoration for his flashy possessions. These individuals often have an obsession with maintaining a certain appearance and react in a highly negative way when their proverbial glass house has been shattered. Usually, the term is defined as an excessive high opinion of one's self which is nothing more than an exaggerated vanity.

Many people with this issue believe themselves to be more supreme to others and can not tolerate individuals who challenge that belief well. Those around them may perceive them with negative connotations, but as long as a vain individual can maintain his or her self opinion, the belief remains intact. The paradox remains that those with a dominant inferiority complex often give the perception of being 'flashier' with material goods while those with a dominant superiority complex may or may not present a 'flashy' appearance. According to Adler, the behavior is not defined by the behavior but rather is defined by self perception. Both an inferiority complex and superiority complex are a result of the same thing—fear.

Ultimately, these individuals will cease to care what others think of them. Vanity also bears a strong relation to illusory superiority in which the individual has become so infatuated with their perception, they refuse to cease in any attempt to convince those who do not share their belief of superiority.

Vanity is not to be confused with a positive level of self-esteem. Those who have a high level of self-esteem do not always go around flashing their few positive attributes but allowing their negative traits to dominate. Those with high self-esteem simply have an unspoken pride and are self-aware of both positive and negative attributes and admit to both. Those who have a tendency to be vain refuse to acknowledge any negative personality traits. It is all about perception.

Speaking of perception and vanity, it is said that those who take excessive 'selfies' may be narcissistic. Selfies are photos that one takes of one's self and are posted to some form of social media such as Facebook, Instagram, Tumblr, or Twitter. There are many other social media platforms, but these four are the most commonly used in regard to selfies and overshare. Many believe that posting excessive selfies is derived from a root need to be noticed and recognized as well as a need to feel attractive. Those who post an excessive amount of selfies tend to seek the approval of others by 'likes' and 'comments' under their pictures. These 'likes' and 'comments' can be seen by others who subsequently end up feeling obligated to either 'like' or 'comment' on the photo as well. How did photos become a symptom of vanity? How did it come to this point in which people's desire to record their own likeness and the likeness of those around them become a psychological disorder? How did such an invention, the camera, lead to such a self-absorbed world?

Smile! Say cheese! Show me those pearly whites! Take a picture! It lasts longer. It is said that a picture is worth a thousand words. Pictures capture memories of events, memories of loved ones, and even can provide a way to keep track of one's ancestry. It is a wonderous and marvelous invention that has evolved exponentially over the years. Brides-to-be contact photographers to capture the moments of their wedding day that they wish to treasure forever. Parents use some form of photography to keep track of their childrens' lives, track growth, and to recall those silly faces their children make. Detectives use photographs to compile evidence against criminals and also to be able to process the crime scene. Regardless of the reasons, the different types of photography allow a person to express their artistic desires as well. Photography is everywhere. From 'selfies' taken and posted on social media to the treasured family photos pasted to old photo albums.

Photography is more than just a hobby. It is a science. The science of photography rests in the procedure for creating photos. Durable images are created by recording a sort of electromagnetic radiation on a light sensitive material. The process is basically this: a lense focuses the light that bounces off of an object on the surface inside the camera during exposure. However, technology has hurled us into the digital age. With digital pictures the same process occurs in a sense; but rather than using a light sensitive surface, the electronic image sensor produces an electrical charge into the individual pixels. Once the charge is produced onto the pixels, it is processed and then immediately stored into a digital image file. Exposure photography is one method of particular interest. However to fully understand exposure photography, one must first understand how the science of photography was developed—no pun intended.

Tools of the Trade

Cameras have been in existence for quite some time, if one were so inclined to think about it truthfully.

The word, photography, comes from the Greek root words photos- and -graphos which mean 'light' and 'drawing', respectively. Yet, many wonder as to the true history of photography. What are its origins? Who was the first person who had a photograph made? What would it have been like to be witness to this new wonder in technology? One could be certain that it was quite the experience to be had. It is said that the first true camera was described by ancient great minds such as Aristotle and Euclid as well as the Chinese philosopher, Mo Di during the fifth century. The pinhole camera is one of the simplest forms of cameras. It is described as having a very small opening at one end in an otherwise 'light tight' box. The way that this type of camera functions is that the light from an object goes through this tiny hole and projects the image, upside down, on the other side of the box. Not long after the pinhole camera came the camera obscura. The camera obscura is very similar to the pinhole camera in functionality, but the physical traits of it are slightly different and the ability to portray the picture with color. Anthemius or Tralles was noted to have used a type of camera as well during some of his experimentation along with Ibn al-Haytham, who was noted to have studied both the pinhole camera and the camera obscura.

From the 19th century studio camera that stood on a tripod and used plates to the box camera mass produced in 1900, cameras have been a wonderful invention. Not long after the box camera of 1900, came the compact folding camera released by Kodak in 1922. One of the first one hundred thirty five cameras called the Leica II was released in 1932, only ten years after Kodak released theirs. Then came the Contax S in 1949, just four years after World War Two. The seventies were a decade filled with more than the consequences of the sixties' drug induced haze. The seventies gave the science of photography the Polaroid Color Pack 80 which was an instant camera released in 1975 followed by the digital camera in 2000 called the Canon Ixus. That same year, Nikon released the Nikon D1 which was the first SLR camera of its kind and was primarily used in photojournalism—specifically sports photography because of its fast shutter speed which allowed it to take better photos of moving subjects. As cell phones evolved, so did the ability to take pictures with one. Though some cell phones had cameras prior to 2010, it was not until 2010 that the first smartphone with a built in camera was able to spread digital photographs in private message formats.

Such that it was from the days of the camera obscura, however, that time passed. It was during the life of Albertus Magnus, who lived between 1193 and 1280, discovered the chemical compound called silver nitrate. Silver nitrate, by itself, is a simple inorganic compound. On the periodic table, it is represented by the symbol $AgNO3$. It is highly versatile and was used in early photography often. It would be nearly three hundred years later before Georg Fabricius who lived from 1516 to 1571 would later discover silver chloride. Both of these materials were used to create photographs during medieval times using primitive methods.

The more reliable methods of photography would not be discovered until early nineteenth century. It became a more desired means to capture images and other media as opposed to having portraits painted and sculptures made of one's self. Granted, most people still preferred paintings and such, but the 1820's proved to be a turning point in the development of photography. The first methods during this time period included the use of photographic plates. In simpler terms, these plates were just the mediums in which the photos were transferred to so that the photograph could be created. It would be a French inventor by the name of Nicephore Niepce who would capture the first surviving photograph in 1827. It was a photograph of a scene from nature and was created using a camera obscura and a lense. This, however, was not an easy process. To develop the photo, it took Niepce several hours, though some believe it took days. The process by which he used at the time, commonly referred to as the bitumen process, was not practical in Niepce's opinion. He sought one that would be more practical. However, Niepce would pass away in 1833 before he was able to perfect the process. Luckily for the rest of the world, he engaged a man by the name of Louis Daguerre to assist in the search of this process. By 1827, the pair had managed to get the process of developing the photos in only three hours, but this still was not satisfactory. Yet, after Niepce's death, Daguerre continued the experiments. He focused on the light sensitive silver halides thus creating the process named for him—the daguerreotype process. The basics of this process were secured by 1837. The daguerreotype process only took ten minutes rather than several hours to process the photo. The earliest photo using this method was taken of an individual in 1838 in Paris. Once word was spread about this marvelous new invention, the country of France paid Daguerre a commission in exchange for permission to present the invention to the world. This happened on August of 1839.

However, seven years earlier and thousands of miles from France, a Brazilian by the name of Hercules Florence was creating his own process. The same year, an Englishman by the name of William Talbot did the same thing. Unfortunately, both men kept theirs a secret until they heard about Daguerre's invention regarding the photography process. Both men set out to improve upon the process, but only Talbot was successful in 1840 with the calotype. Talbot's process created what is known today as 'negatives'. These 'negatives' were translucent and could be used to create additional 'positive' copies whereas the daguerreotype could only be reproduced by taking the photo again with the people in the same poses.

Just before Talbot released his calotype in 1840, his process was taken one step further with improvements which resulted in what is known as cyanotype, or blueprints. This was done by John Herschel in 1839 when the first glass negative was created. As time continued, more discoveries in the world of photography would come to existence—especially in 1851. That was the year for the ambrotype, the ferrotype (or tintype as more commonly known), and again the glass negative. The tintype, or ferrotype, was one of the most commonly preferred by soldiers during the civil war. Since the images were projected on metal, they had a tendency to last longer through the toils of the battlefield.

It was not until 1891 that the next development in photography would take place. Gabriel Lippmann invented a new process for making photographs containing natural color based on interference of light waves. This eventually led to his nomination and achievement of the Nobel Peace Price in Physics in 1908.

Film Photography

In 1876, work was began on light sensitive photographic emulsions. Photographic emulsions are colloids that are light sensitive. They are made up of silver halide crystals and gelatin. Ferdinand Hurter and Vero Charles Driffield, both scientists, used the processes of sensitometry and densitometry to create what is known as an actinograph. This was the first development in film photography.

An actinograph is one of the instruments used by Hurter and Driffield to measure the amount of light available—or rather, measured the chemical intensity of light. This was used in opposition of measuring radiometric or photometric light. One of the earliest actinographs included a recording device with a twenty four hour capacity. A rotating cylinder of photographic paper was exposed through a slit that was wedge shaped to record actinic light during a specific part of the day. In 1888, the pair later obtained a patent for their device which estimated the power of sunlight and calculated its power for the purpose of computing exposure time based on plate speed. It also calculated the time of day, time of year and even latitude. Though this was one of the first developments in film photography, it also served as a basis for Arthur Clayden's 1911 version for meteorologists so that they could measure the change of radiation.

George Eastman created on of the first flexible film rolls in 1885. Though the film was nothing more than a coating on paper, it would allow the layer that contained the image to be stripped from that paper and placed on a hardened gelatin support Four years later in 1889, nitrate film was developed using nitrocellulose.

It would still be another twenty years before Kodak would introduce nitrate film, but it still heralded very few uses as nitrate film was quite hazardous. This led to x-ray film in 1933, but nitrate films would remain in use for film photography until 1951.

Still, the movie camera (also known as a video camera) was a camera with the functionality of taking a rapid succession of various photographs and imprinted on a recording medium. These series of images were called 'frames'. In order to achieve this, there was a specialized mechanism inside the camera that determined the rate of speed in which the frames were recorded, thus also controlling the images as they were played back. When the frame rate was also input into a playback device, it caused the person's biological components of both the brain and they eyes to be able to cause the photos to merge thus creating the illusion of motion.

Black and White Photography Versus Color

Originally, all photographs were monochromatic. This meant that all photos were in a 'black and white' format. Many people enjoyed the lower cost of black and white and the quality of a classic look to it. Black and white photography's characteristics are that the tones between darker areas and lighter areas within the photograph. This does not mean that the only two colors within a black and white photograph are limited to only black or white, though over exposure and under exposure would lead to that result. It includes the shades of the two. The process in which the photographs are developed are important as well. For example, the cyanotypes typically come out with more bluish tones than black, white, or gray and the albumin process is what creates the sepia tints in photographs.

To date, well processed silver halide based materials are still available and a lot of photographers use these materials to create monochromatic images per the request of a particular client. As a matter of fact, some digital cameras are created so that they create solely monochromatic pictures. The process for creating a monochromatic picture is also advantageous when some color photographs are in need of salvaging. Monochromatic pictures are also considered an art form, despite the availability of color.

Color photography was first experimented with during the 1840's, but that process was not a favorable one at the time. The reason it was not favorable was that the color faded all too quickly once the photograph was exposed to 'white light'. However in 1861 near the beginning of the

American Civil War, a physicist by the name of James C. Maxwell took three separate photographs of the same image. The first time, he used a red filter. The second time, he used a green filter. The third time, he used a blue filter. This process allowed him the three color channels required to make one color photograph.

During that same decade, Louis Ducos du Hauron pioneered a process for superimposing carbon prints for projection screens. Sergei Mikhailovich Prokudin-Gorskii, however, made the most use from Maxwell and du Hauron's technique using a special camera. Though the technique did not result in perfect pictures if the subject moved around a lot, but it was successful.

Color photography was not widely used because of the sensitivity of some of the materials, and it did not begin to evolve sufficiently until the photochemist Hermann Vogel discovered sensitization of dye in 1873. His early processes are what led to color photography having any sort of commercial viability.

In 1907, the Lumière brothers introduced their creation—autochrome. Autochrome is a process in which mosaic-style colored filters are incorporated via plates creating a positive transparency. This process filled the gap in color photography between the 1890's and 1950's. Using this process, Kodak eventually introduced the 'monopack' color film in 1935. It used all three major color components through the process of a multi-layer emulsion. This was called 'Kodachrome'. Agfacolor Neu, used a similar process, but simplified the process by incorporating the emulsion layers during manufacturing. To follow up with both Kodak and

Agfacolor Neu's processes, Polaroid created a camera in 1963 that would produce color photographs with only a one to two minute exposure. This development was one of the most important developments in regard to mainstreaming photography. Soon after this camera was released for public consumption, everyone had the ability to take photographs without having to have them developed in special locations or build what was known as a 'darkroom' in order to develop pictures. This also led to the mainstreaming of slide projection. Soon, families would record the events of their special moments, vacations, or births of children and have those images developed on to positive transparencies on special paper. In addition to that, it also led to the introduction of automatic photo printing equipment and one hour photo shops.

The year 1981 was a major year for the art of photography as it was that year Sony introduced the first camera that used a charge coupled device for imaging. This was important because it eradicated the need for traditional film strips. This device was called the Sony Mavica. It saved images to a disk and displayed them on televisions. Though not fully digital, it paved the way for Kodak's DCS100 model ten years later. The DCS100 contained a single lens. This model of camera also introduced the concept of digital photography and paved the way for photojournalism's introduction to mainstream.

Parts of a Camera

One of the most important and obvious tools of a photographer is the camera. While there are many, many different styles in existence and have been over the centuries, the basic concepts and parts remain the same. Some of the most important things a photographer should know about are: focus, aperture, shutter speed, white balance, metering, ISO speed, Autofocus point, focal length, and filters.

As one adjusts the opening of the lense, this is called focusing as it allows more or less light to pass through the lense as desired. This opening itself is called the aperture, which affects field depth and diffraction. Often one seeks to control the speed in which the image is exposed to light. This is the shutter speed. The faster the shutter speed, the less likely the image risks coming out blurry.

Digital cameras give a sort of compensation for the temperature of the color with a specified set of lighting conditions. Basically, this is ensuring that the white light is registered and the frame appears natural. The process for mechanical cameras is slightly different as this is controlled by the type of film one uses. Many people recall those long, rectangle cameras that often required one to take the film to the store and wait for it to be developed at the photo shop. The film one would use in that camera was often denoted with something similar to the number three hundred or four hundred followed by the word exposure which constituted the specific white balance of the film. This allowed the photographer to ensure that the exposure of the highlights and shadows met his or her wishes. This specific process was called metering and was often done with a separate device called a 'light metering device'. Sometimes, the photographer would not need this device if his or her skill was good enough in order for the correct settings to be gauged. ISO speed is a functionality of the camera. What happens involving the ISO speed is that this 'tells' the camera what the film speed is. Thi higher the number, the more sensitive to light the film is. If one is able to gauge the correct combination of the afforementioned functions, the film is considered to be correctly exposed.

Digital cameras often had CMOS technology as well as the CCD. CMOS stands for complementary metal oxide semiconductor. This technology is useful for its results in digital cameras. It is a type of technology that allows the construction of integrated circuits. This technology uses a mostly symmetrical pair of MOSFETs, or metal oxide semiconductor field effect transistors. What these transistors do is that they allow low power consumption as well as an immunity to high levels of noise. As a result, there is not a lot of heat waste as with other forms which tend to have current flow regardless of it being out of the changing state.

The manner of which these circuits are created requires that there be some sort of input from a voltage source or something similar. Another option for power source is called a PMOS transistor. With the PMOS, the amount of resistance a current will face is remarkably low. However, the metal oxide semiconductor field effect transistors create a level of high resistance between the source and the drain.

The final result in this is that the output of both transistors compliment the desired function with the design of it since the input is high and the output is at a lower threshold which reduces the amount of energy necessary. Yet, there is a duality that exists between the two. The curcuit path exists from the output to the ground or the output to the power source. It uses De Morgan's laws of logic as for one, there is a parallel of the other.

Less power is wasted with a static CMOS as opposed to the NMOS only because the power with the former is depleted only when it is switching. It is a process of ninety nanometers. The reason that the NMOS is the less desirable of the two functions is that there is always a current that travels through the load resistor which creates the drain on the power.

There is a proven idea behind static dissipation. What happens is that first, there must be a gate source threshold voltage. This means that the current through the device will drop significantly due to static dissipation.

On occassion, there were situations in which leakage occurred as a result of a type of reverse bias between the wells and the diffusion regions. Beacuse these leakages are so small, they are often omitted in the calculations of the power required by the device.

Charge coupled devices, similar to the CMOS wiring, moves electrical charges like any other power transistor set up. However, this usually happens in devices that allow the charge to be converted into digital values or manipulated. This is the primary device within digital cameras because the image sensors are represented by MOS capacitors which exist above the threshold for inversion. This allows the conversion of photons that are incoming to be converted to electron charges. The charge coupled device reads these charges. They also allow for different types of light detection such as infrared or ultraviolet light and are preferred among those in the medical, scientific, and professional photography communities.

The charge coupled device was initially created in 1969 by AT&T and were originally called 'charge bubble devices'. Memory, delay lines, and imaging devices were included in the initla paper that described the concept within the labs as Michael Tompsett was assigned the project. In the first experiments, a row of metal squares that were closely spaced were accessed by bonds of wire on top of an oxidized silicon surface. With the first working versions of the device, a very simplified version of an eight bit shift register was included in integration. This particular build was essentially a rustic eight pixel device. Tompsett's continued efforts caused the development of this device to progress at an alarmingly rapid rate of speed. By the time 1971 came around, more and more images were able to be captured. RCA, Texas Instruments, and other major electronic firms sought out and began their own development programs based on Tompsett's design. In 1974, Gil Amelio created a two dimensional one hundred by one hundred pixel device based on Tomsett's design. One year later, the first digital camera was born followed by the KH-11 Kennan reconnaissance satellite which was released into orbit in 1976. By the early eighties, Sony was using the charge coupled devices inside of their camcorders.

In regard to awards for achievement, The National Academy of Engineering Charles Stark Draper Prize was given to Boyle and Smith— two scientists who aided in the development of this technology. Also, the Nobel Peace Prize in Physics was awarded to the pair in 2009 as well. For his contribution, Michael Tompsett was given the 2010 National Medal of Technology.

As the technology further developed still, digital color cameras were developed with what is called a Bayer mask that is placed over the charge coupled device. The reason is that since the human eye is more sensitive to the color green than it is to blue or red, the luminance information is collected through each pixel which allows for the color resolution to be lower than the luminance. However, there are some with better charge coupled devices. Rather it is not necessarily a better version of the one, but a layer of three in addition to a dichroic beam splitter prism. This beam splitter prism splits the image up into the three main color components of red, blue, and green. This technique is primarily used on camcorders, but also applies to some digital cameras.

In microscopy, the Bayer mask's resolution is often enhanced through a microscanning process in which a production of several frames of the particular scene are created. The sensor is moved through the dimensions of the pixels. The purpose for this is to allow each individual point in the visual field to be acquired consecutively.

Sensors for the charge coupled device come in many different sizes. The sizes are referred to as the optical format, but are measured in fractions of an inch.

Once the exposure is considered to be 'long enough', an overflow of sorts will take place primarily with the brightest part of the image. This process, called blooming, is the end result of this process. This is not a favored result. So, to combat this result, anti-blooming features are available to the charge coupled devices in order to reduce the sensitivity to a specific light form. This creates a drain structure by reducing the sensitivity of the pixel area.

Further still, there is an L3Vision charge coupled device in existence. What happens with this particular device is that the gain register is placed center between the shift and the output. Large stages, made up of gain registers, are multiplied by a process called impact ionization. An avalanche diode is similar to this as well. Intensified charge coupled devices have a gain that is considered to be stochastic.

Still, one need not be overwhelmed at the technicalities involved with photography. Though there are more techniques and other things involved in photography that equates more than simply to point and click one's camera at an object, it is still an enjoyable hobby for most. Even children are capable of taking a proper photograph.

Some cameras have an ability to 'auto focus'. This means that there is a system inside of the camera that allows it to, once the target is selected, focus in on that object automatically. Most cameras with single lenses have this ability.

The focal length is determined by the length of the lens itself. For example, a photographer may install an additional lense on the front of the camera such as a wide angle lense, a fisheye, or zoom lens.

Through most of this book, you have been told about the different color filters in some of the older models of cameras, specifically during the American Civil War era. The filters are often placed between the object being photographed and the material recording the light—usually in front of the lens. However, it can also be placed at the rear of the lens.

Sensitivity of the light is in regard to the intensity of the light, color, and wavelengths. Most of the time, this is measured in pixels or grains of the silver halide combination. However, one of the more important elements of photography is defining the f-number. The larger the aperture is equal to a smaller f-number. An international convention seeking to create an 'across the board' system standardized this idea. As the f-number is decreased, it is done so by a factor of the square root of the number two. This means that if the diameter of the aperture is increased by the same number theory, but in factors of the number two rather than its square root. For example, going up one notch increases the amount of light reaching the film via the aperture by double. A longer lens equates to less of the image being in focus. This also means that shorter lenses equal more of the image being in the focus.

Capturing the image is only part of the photographic process. It is imperative that, despite the material used, the process itself is required to capture the image desired and create a viewable image. In regard to slides, the film is mounted on a specified mount so that it can be used in a projector. Photographs, since the 1960's, require the development of a film negative by printing it out on special paper. Before the inventions of laser jet printers and inkjet printers, the desired negatives could be mounted inside of an enlarger. An enlarger is just that—a machine that increases the size of the photograph by projecting it onto light sensitive paper. After the photo was enlarged, it would be soaked in a sort of chemical 'bath' and then transferred to what is called a 'stop bath'. This stop bath would stop the process of development and prevent it from exposing any further once light was introduced to the photograph. Then, the photograph would be literally hung out to dry. Many traditional style hobbyists still employ this technique in order to develop their photos, but the wide availability of digital cameras and digital imagery has taken first place in most used techniques because of the ease in which the photographic file can be transferred from the camera to a computer or digital image server such as a picture sharing website like Instagram or Tumblr. The ease at which these digital photograph files can be printed and reprinted is why this form is so widely used.

Techniques

There are so many different techniques in which to produce a final product—i.e the photograph. Contrast alters the visual properties of specific images. This allows the particular object to become more distinguished from the other objects as well as the background. Dodging reduces exposure which causes certain areas to be lighter than the others. 'Burning in' is the opposite of Dodging. 'Burning in' adds more exposure so that areas will appear darker.

Most people are familiar with the texture of the paper in which one prints their photos. Most photos now are done on a high gloss sheet which gives it the 'shine' most see on pictures. Other paper textures in addition to glossy are ones such as 'matte'. Matte is not as shiny and keeps the reflection of the light from being a distraction from appreciating the photograph. To take it one step further, one must also decide on the type of paper one wishes to use. Do you prefer a resin coated paper, which is smooth, or a fiber based type of paper? Then, finally, one must decide on the size of the paper thus also deciding on the size of the photograph copy one wishes. Most photograph packages offered in places such as Sears or Wal-Mart include pictures that are eight inches in width and ten inches in height. Finally, the exposure shape should be chosen. Do you want a print that is in a circle, oval, or traditional rectangle?

Some other techniques include what is called three dimensional imaging or stereoscopy. For example, monochromatic and autochromatic pictures can be displayed side by side in a panoramic view similar to that of a typical human stereoscopic vision. Most people think of three dimensional as being life-like. However, in photography, it is more of the panoramic view that defines stereoscopy.

Full Spectrum, Light Field Photography, and More...

For several decades, since the 1960's, other types of photography styles have been employed including ultraviolet and infrared films. Since the birth of digital photography, this full spectrum photography avenue has led to new artistic styles.

Some digital cameras have been modified to detect some levels of ultraviolet light. However, most digital cameras straight off of the shelf contain a hot mirror. This infrared hot mirror is a filter that blocks most of the infrared spectrum narrowing it from four hundred to approximately seven hundred nanometers.

As a person replaces the hot mirror, also known as the infrared blocking filter, with an infrared pass called a wide spectrally transmitting filter will then allow the camera to 'see' the different lights with more ease. Though these methods are great for fine art photography, geologists, forensic scientists, and law enforcement officials have found uses for it as well.

Synthetic aperture photography is a method of capturing images and processing displays by varying the depts of the field after the capture of the photograph. In 1846, Michael Faraday explained that the light field is a five dimensional space that has the attributes of more angles. It is defined by the direction of the rays that pass through a specific point in that light field.

As previously mentioned, there were some of the earlier experimentations in photography that led to the creation of x-ray technology around the end of the nineteenth century. That technology led to other methods of forming images with light such as photocopying or xerography which are forms of electrophotography. In this process, machines form images on specialized transparent paper by the use and transfer of static electrical charges. These 'photograms' of sorts are produced by the shadows left behind by these charges which create the image.

Amateur photography and commercial photography are both considered art forms, but commercial photographers take their love of capturing images and turn it into monetary profit. A commercial photographer has so many avenues in which to turn a profit with this art form. For advertisers, packshots are taken for the purpose to sell the product or service. Think of how the image of a soda can on a bill board generates interest in that particular brand of product.

Some people have an appealing enough physique to be considered models. Most people are familiar with names such as Calvin Klein or Tacori (jewelry). These brands use models which have created fashion and glamour photography as a form of advertising. This form of advertising uses the models to create a buzz of sorts about the product in order to get consumers to desire said product. In glamour photography, nude models are also used to sell things such as magazines. An example of this would be Maxim or Playboy magazine.

Earlier, it was mentioned how infrared and ultraviolet photography assisted with law enforcement. To expand further on this concept, another style of commercial photography is called crime scene photography. Part of processing a crime scene involves taking photographs of that crime scene which includes the following: the body of the victim in a murder or photos of bruises and cuts of an assault victim, the area in which the crime was committed which may show details of the identity of the criminal, and any other information that would be helpful to solving said crime.

Have you ever seen an advertisement for a circus depicting the animals and the acrobats involved which made you want to attend that circus? Circus photography is its own classification under commercial photography. Though it is a form of advertisement, it requires a specialized set of skills using high shutter speeds with very low light. It also requires skills in which the photographer must be able to capture a trick or an act in the matter of a split second, similar to that of sports photography in which the same skills must be employed.

Still life photography is a simple concept. It involves photos taken of inanimate objects such as furniture, appliances, or even food items for the purpose of advertisement. Think of the pictures of washing machines or dryers you see in the inserts in a newspaper or the billboard with a picture of a hamburger from a local fast food restaurant. These are examples of still life. However food photography, which is a part of still life photography, but requires an additional skill set.

Photojournalism is a style of editorial photography. Photojournalists take pictures of news events to emphasize the premise of the story. For example, photojournalists during the Vietnam war often took picutres of war-torn villages, children starving, or even pictures of the fields of dead from both sides. Paparazzi are extremists in the photojournalism world. These individuals will do anything and go anywhere to capture actors, politicians, and other prominent individuals in very candid (and sometimes risque) positions. Most view them as trash talkers and no better than tabloid magazines. However, it has been said that paparrazi were responsible for the death of England's favorite princess, Princess Diana. She was being followed by paparrazi as she was on an evening out with what is believed to be her lover. The paparrazi left no room to maneuver as they chased the couple into that fateful tunnel where the car wreck happened.

It is said that pictures are worth a thousand words—at least according to that particular aphorism. Photojournalists take this to the extreme. The magazine, National Geographic, is a magazine with great articles but is also primarily a magazine with a focus on photojournalism. Also, a form of wildlife photography is used in this same magazine. This is almost as dangerous as photojournalism, but more so in my opinion. Some of the animals that are photographed are quite dangerous, and those same animals do not discriminate when it comes to attacking you if provoked. Think about the photos of bears, lions, or other dangerous animals you have seen in magazines. National Geographic also contains pictures of sharks. In order for those photos to be taken, someone has to get into a wetsuit, be lowered into the ocean in a shark cage (and not all of the shark photographers took the pictures from a cage), and use the special camera to capture the beasts in their environments. Of course, the more peaceful version of this is pet photography.
Some people view their pets as 'fur babies' or furry, four legged children

and have pictures taken of their pets.

Renoir painted landscapes. Some people take pictures of landscapes with the same premise—artistic views of a specific landscape. However, landscape photography is considered more so to be a form of commercial photography. Landscape photography can be used to advertise a location such as a plantation for those who desire antebellum weddings or even book covers.

Speaking of weddings, almost every wedding has a photographer on hand to record those precious moments of the families celebrating a union between their loved ones. Sometimes, the photographer will create slide shows or even enlist videography to record the events. Also, wedding photographers will sometimes seek the permission of the wedding party to use their photos for the purpose of advertising their services. The market for the services a commercial photographer provides is quite expansive and is unlikely that the demand will dissipate in the slightly distant future.

Artistically speaking, the antithesis of commercial photography is photography that is done for aesthetic purposes. Though it is not a complete opposite in technique, the purpose is what defines them as an opposite. The twentieth century has seen a boom of artistic photography as the technology has become available. Such notable people as Edward Weston, Alfred Stieglitz, Edward Steichen, John Szarkowski, and F. Holland Day have brought about the sub-categories of fine art photography and documentary photography to the artistic world of gallery art. Some of these notables first attempted what is called pictorialism, or the imitation of painting styles. In this form, a softer focus is used for the purpose of creating an almost 'hazy' or 'dreamy' look. Other notables such as Ansel Adams preferred to advocate what was referred to as 'straight photography'. This style of artistic photography focuses on the object being photographed itself rather than forcing it to imitate something other than what it is.

The different art forms of photography has been a subject matter that is often discussed. Some feel that it is too mechanical of a representation and has very little artistic value while others say that it is an art form of itself. Those proponents of the latter feel that capturing an item or event and being able to elicit an emotional response from a person is what constitutes it as an art form. To paraphrase Clive Bell's essay titled 'Art', he states that no work of art should be considered worthless as the definition of art is subjective. It changes along with perception of the individual as well as the perception of the society in which the art is created. To expand further on his concept, imagine how Daguerre and Niepce's work was looked upon during the time in which both men lived. Though at the time, many did not consider it an art form. However looking back upon their work, many today would consider it for the artistic value it possesses.

Science and the Camera

Cameras have been used in scientific explorations and recordings since Daguerre's time. Some have used it to record solar and lunar eclipses while others have used it to record the existence of certain creatures and plants for the purpose of later identification. As a matter of fact, the recording of certain creatures and plants led to the creation of two other sub-categories in photography: photomicroscopy and macrophotography. With photomicroscopy, the camera is attached to the microscope at the eye piece in order to record microscopic cells. This is how some photos in science books were taken. Macrophotography is for recording larger creatures and plants.

Cameras often aid in law enforcement, as previously mentioned. Forensic photography is a field in which the individual records crime scenes with the photographs which are later used when the case is presented in court. One such example is in a murder. Usually, the position of the body and the area around the body is photographed. This has even led to establishing whether a serial killer was the one behind the murder or whether the murder was a result of a one time killer. Some television series, though a fantasy story which often does not truthfully depict what really happens in life, have managed to get some things correct in regard to crime scene photography. For example, forensic psychiatrists can look at a string of crime scene photos in order to aid in creating a profile of the killer. This is often done when a serial killer is suspected to be responsible. Theodore 'Ted' Bundy was actually profiled using this technique. Some serial killers position the bodies in a specific way or leave behind a specific 'calling card', as it were. Forensic photography allows for this type of information to be tracked and provides evidence of certain theories in regard to the crime.

Photography is not always as innocent of a profession or hobby as it is portrayed. Photography has a dark side. In 1954, Alfred Hitchcock introduced this concept into mainstream society through his movie titled 'Rear Window'. It was believed that his film promoted the use of cameras in voyeurism, though that is not the case. A quote from Michael Powell's 'Peeping Tom', a movie produced in 1960, is paraphrased by saying that the camera is not that which commits the crime itself. It can, however, record the crime through the acts of instrusion or even exploitation. In 'Peeping Tom', images of pain and suffering were captured during the commission of certain sadistic and sexually violent crimes.

In today's digital age, photographs can be easily manipulated or 'photoshopped' to create a false representation of its object. However, the cameras used in forensic photography produce a sort of digital fingerprint that cannot be duplicated in order to prevent and detect tampering of the photos.

Exposure Photography

Thus far, the history and styles of photography has been explained in a one sided discussion form. Yet, one of the most interesting forms of photography yet to be introduced is exposure photography, though the basic forms of the concept have been mentioned. One such concept is specifically exposure. Exposure is best described as the amount of light reaching the film. It is determined by many different factors such as the aperture of the lense, the shutter speed, and the amount of light reflecting off the object or at the scene. This is the essence of what is called the shutter cycle. Photometric exposure is the amount of light that is visible, or light energy, in the area of a surface in a specific amount of time. The equation representing this statement is:

$H_v = E_v \cdot t$

The symbols in this equation are as follows whereas the letter H_v represents the end result which is the photometric exposure. E_v is equal to the amount of light in the scene or coming from the object. The lowercase 't' represents time measured in seconds. Sometimes, the radiometric quantity is used instead. It is similar to this particular equation, however it us the product of irradiance rather than luminosity. Most materials of a photographic nature are sensitive to what is considered 'invisible' light such as ultraviolet or infrared light. This can be both a benefit or a nuisance depending on the desired results of the photographer.

Ultraviolet light, in regard to photography, is a benefit to some photographers. Normally, the glass lenses of cameras block the radiation from ultraviolet light. Sometimes, outdoor photographers use ultraviolet blocking filters, but those that do not wish to block the ultraviolet light tend to utilize quartz lenses that are created just for that purpose. What purpose does ultraviolet photography serve? Normally, ultraviolet photography is only used in a commercial capacity such as the fields of medicine, science, and forensics.

Ultraviolet photography in the forensic field is probably the most well known method as far as common knowledge goes. Imagine that a police officer has been called to a crime scene. The coroner is called out and the crime scene unit processes the whole area taking fibers, hair, looking for DNA, as well as taking pictures of the area. The body is taken to the coroner's office for further processing. The coroner will use a camera with the special quartz lense to look for bruises that have yet to surface. The reason is that when blood vessels are forced to burst underneath the skin, which is what a bruise is in the most basic form, it takes a few moments for those bruises to surface and show on the skin. Using an ultraviolet camera can detect these bruises before they've had a chance to surface—bruises that are usually made pre-mortem. This ability to detect under the surface bruises in this way help aid in the estimation of the time of death of the victim because it takes a specific amount of time for bruises to come to the surface—usually a few minutes. So, with this technology and if such bruises are detected, the coroner will be able to determine what time the victim died which will allow the law enforcement officers to begin ruling out or include certain persons of interest to determine whether those people are upgraded to suspect or discarded altogether.

In the field of science, without getting very specific in regard to which particular field, ultraviolet photography allows scientists to take pictures of anything from the Aurora at the north pole of Jupiter from space to pictures of individual cells. It also allows astronomers to determine the chemical compositions of certain interstellar bodies.

Commercial photographers are more than just amateurs who happen to make money doing what they love. Although some are lucky to be no more than just an amateur who has a knack for marketing, most true commercial photographers are well aware of the logarithmic scales that apply to the sensitometric data which expresses log exposure. Some such quantities of photometry units are the following: luminous energy (Q_v), luminous flux (Φ_v), luminous intensity (I_v), luminance (L_v), illuminance (E_v), luminous emittance (M_v), and luminous exposure (H_v), as well as others.

Luminous energy is calculated in lumen seconds or talbots. Luminous power, also known as luminous flux is calculated by lumens. Luminous intensity is meansured in candelas while luminance is measured as a candela per square meter. Illuminance, which is not the same as luminance, serves the purpose of detecting incidents on surfaces and is measured in lux.

Sensitometry is a science of its own. There is a technical approach that recognizes the useful exposure range's physical limitations. Also called a dynamic range, this approach states that if film is exposed to light outside of this range of specifications, the subject of the photograph will not be recorded accurately. In regard to a black and white photo, an overexposure or underexposure will cause the different graduated shades of the color and tone required of an authentic black and white photograph to be recorded in *only* black or white. Sometimes overexposure or underexposure can be beneficial, despite popular belief of the contrary. For example, imagine that a photo has been taken of a young child receiving confirmation in the Catholic church. The priest is wearing his usual white altar cloth, but the cloth is more of an 'off-white'--a color it should not be. A photographer may use the overexposure or underexposure process in order to make the cloth appear perfectly white.

Speaking of science, one cannot properly detail the ins and outs of photography without recognizing a scientist who, in 1853, took the science applied in photography and created a plethora of instruments that measured and recorded their readings by a photographic process. That scientist is Charles Brooke. He invented instruments such as barometers, thermometers, psychrometers, and magnetometers. Charles Brooke was not only an inventor, he was a physician. More specifically, he was a surgeon.

Born in 1804, Brooks was the son of an affluent mineralogist. Since his family was well off, he was afforded several opportunities that are said to have attributed to his success as well as his intellect. He studied under some of the most reputable physicians of the time such as Dr. Turner. Later, he spent five years at St. John's College in Cambridge with his professional education in medicine ending with St. Bartholomew's Hospital and successful completion in testing with the Royal College of Surgeons. One of his most famous techniques in medicine was when he developed the 'bead suture' which aided in the treatment of deeper lacerations. However, his passion rested within other scientific inventions particularly in the field of meteorology and in connections with the Royal Botanical Society.

What led him to create his afforementioned inventions was his study in physics and mathematics as most of the public papers he wrote and the lectures he gave were on those subjects. One of his most noted papers was titled, '*Motion of Sound in Space*'. This paper was the catalyst which led to his inventions. These inventions (barometer, thermometers, psychrometers, and magnetometers) produced results which were measured using photography. While he studied the theory of microscopes, which also uses a form of photography when capturing the images of microscopic organisms or items on a cellular level, he did create some inventions that led to the official creation of the microscope people are more familiar with today by the shifting of lenses that improved illumination.

During the years of 1846 and 1852, Brooke was at his most productive in regard to the previously mentioned inventions. To record the findings of these instruments, rather to fascilitate their ability to self record, he used a coal/gasoline light source in coordination with mirrors and other optics. This was done with a clockwork drum that had a covering of specialized photographic paper. The mirrors and optics amplified the readings in order for them to be registered properly. Many of these inventions were sought after and regailed as modern miracles of science as well as adopted by several meteorological stations from several places around the world. The Smithsonian Institute built upon Brooke's design in 1859 along with the Coast Survey (that period's Coast Guard).

Though there were other magnetometers between 1850 and 1850, Charles Brooke's device was the logest lasting and most stable version at the time. As a matter of fact, in 1859, it was Brooke's device located at the Kew Observatory that recorded two of the largest terrestrial magnetic storms in history. These events, the Stewart Super Flare and the Carrington Super Flare, reached the Earth in September of 1859.

As mentioned, the science of photography led to the creation of the x-ray.

The laws governing anything pertaining to photography are fairly complex. A person can gain a copyright to a photo as long as they have permission of the subject of the photo (assuming the subject is a person with the legal capabilities to enter into a contract or is represented by another individual with such rights). Due to many terrorism laws, some countries have placed restrictions on photographers on taking certain pictures in specific public places without consent from the government.

A multitude of photography styles, particularly exposure photography, have been explored in the text above. The history, the science, and the many uses along with the legal matters pertaining to photography have been explored. Photography is much more than simply picking up a camera, peering through the lens, aiming at a subject, pointing, and clicking the shutter. The process is a scientifically designed one involving apertures, shutter speeds, luminosity, and focus. A photograph can be ruined by overexposure or underexposure as well as made phenomenal by the same process. Perhaps the human desire for vanity and creating an image of one's self led to the invention of the camera, or perhaps it was the desire to record our lives for posterity. No one person can be certain about the reasons as those reasons are atttributed to a society which is made up of many people. In most society's, the majority rules and decides what is accepted and desired by the whole group. It is a theory, though not an incredibly popular one, that the reason photography changed so much and gained so much recognition during the time of the American Civil War was that this was the first war that tore apart families on such a grand scale. Many men had tintype photographs made with their families as they prepared to join their local militia or join up with the Union Army with fear that the time they would be away from home was uncertain. Though many gave off an air of over-confidence, most feared the worst—never being able to return. So, they wanted to create physical manifestations of memories.

The demand for this is what led to the creation and development of the supply. Regardless, the wonderous invention of photography was invented and later, successfully made it to the 'Main Street Society', or basically ended up in every home before electricity. No one ever imagined the results and consequences of the development of the camera nor did anyone ever contemplate how exposure photography morphing into digital photography would affect society on the whole. Now, nearly everyone— even most children—has some form of camera in their hands. Most of those cameras are attached to their smart phones, thus created the beginning of YouTube videos of teens fighting in a 'fight club' style, challenges such as the ice bucket challenge for ALS (also known as Lou Gherig's disease), and other seriously disturbing things or pictures. Teens are now sending provocative text images, or multimedia messages, and society has seemed to turn toward a darker path. Though exposure photography and digital photography serve a positive purpose, the law has yet to catch up. Let us hope this trend ceases and desist and people regain their sense of responsibility.